JUSTIN BIEBER

Oh Boy!

Publisher and Creative Director: Nick Wells
Project Editors: Polly Prior and Catherine Taylor
Picture Research: Laura Bulbeck and Alex McClean
Art Director and Layout Design: Mike Spender
Digital Design and Production: Chris Herbert

Special thanks to: Stephen Feather, Daniela Nava and Tony Phillips

FLAME TREE PUBLISHING
Crabtree Hall, Crabtree Lane
Fulham, London SW6 6TY
United Kingdom

www.flametreepublishing.com

First published 2012

12 14 16 15 13
3 5 7 9 10 8 6 4

Flame Tree Publishing is an imprint of Flame Tree Publishing Ltd

© 2012 Flame Tree Publishing Ltd

A CIP record for this book is available from the British Library upon request.

ISBN 978-0-85775-278-9

Printed in China

JUSTIN BIEBER

Oh Boy!

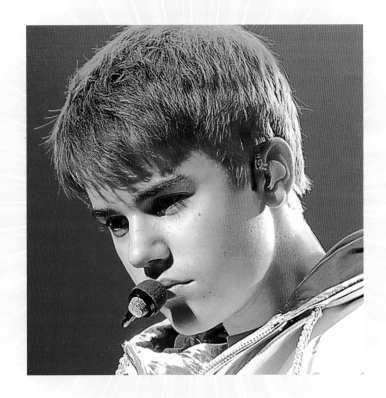

NADIA COHEN

FOREWORD: MANGO SAUL, EDITOR, SUGARSCAPE.COM

**FLAME TREE
PUBLISHING**

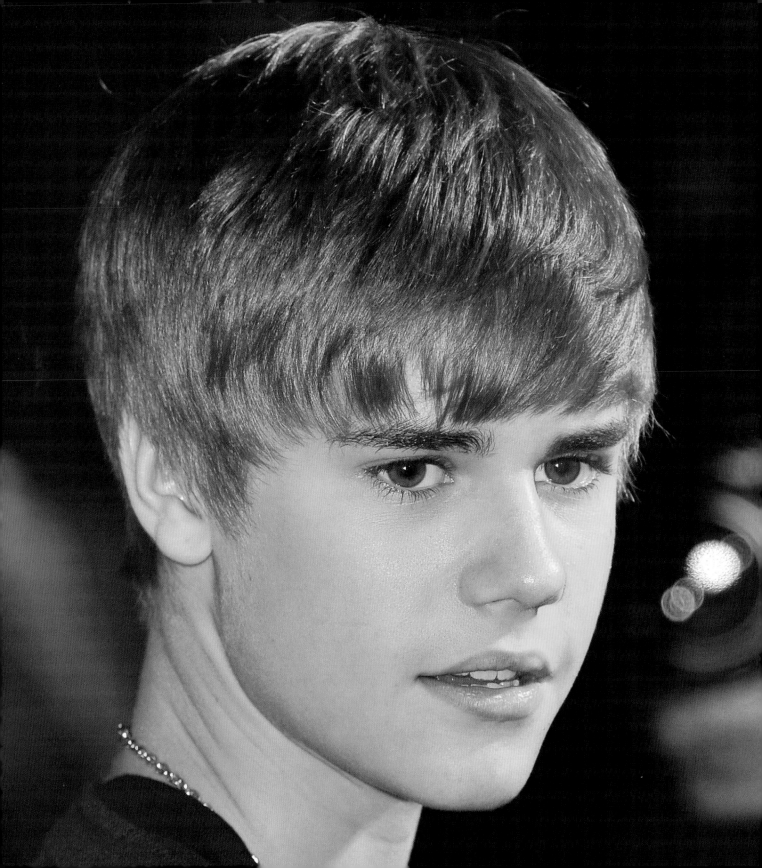

Contents

Foreword

'Hello? Hello? I can't hear you. In fact I can't hear anything...' Serves me right for picking up the phone whilst attending the premiere of Justin Bieber's DVD *Never Say Never* at the O2 in London. I think you could hear the screaming Beliebers in Scotland. Loud is not the word. Think a rocket a few metres from your face. Luckily, with this book, you can get the best of Bieber up close and personal with the singer himself and without having to damage your eardrums!

There will be a recurring theme in this Foreword and this book in general. Vast, massive, huge, mammoth and all the related synonyms you can find in a thesaurus. Love him or hate him, you can't dismiss the fact that Justin Bieber is the biggest pop star on the planet. For a 17-year-old who only started uploading his bedroom acoustic performances to YouTube a few years ago, that's a mean feat.

We need to understand how big Justin Bieber is and this fact might get some sort of perspective. His videos on YouTube have been watched over two billion times. That's big considering there are seven billion people on planet Earth. There are more Bieber-related facts that make your eyeballs pop out, but you'll have to delve into this awesome book to find out. So, what are you waiting for? Get yourself a hot beverage, preferably with some sort of biscuit with chocolate smeared all over it and get stuck in...

Mango Saul, Editor, www.sugarscape.com

Record Sales

Although he only turned 17 in 2011, it already seems impossible to imagine a world without Justin Bieber in it. Since 'One Time', the first single from Justin's debut album, was released in July 2009, he has catapulted into superstardom at such a phenomenal speed that even his most devoted fans have been left quite breathless. 'One Time' reached the Top 20 in five countries and, before he knew it, Justin had become the first solo artist in history to have at least four singles enter the Top 40 prior to his debut album's release.

When his first album *My World* was released in November 2009, it sold 137,000 copies in its first week, but went on to peak at No. 6 on the US *Billboard* chart. It debuted at No. 1 in Canada and less than two months later had sold over 1 million copies in the States. It sold almost 2 million copies worldwide and here in the UK it was certified double platinum by the end of 2010, when sales soared after he performed on *The X Factor* results show. It was his first mainstream appearance this side of the Atlantic and we had our initial glimpse of what makes Mr Beiber such a superstar. As he told *X Factor* host Dermot O'Leary, 'I wasn't that nervous; I was pretty cool, pretty calm and collected.'

Justin proved he is not one to rest easy and released the chart-topping *My World 2.0* in 2010. 2011 was a busy year, with *Never Say Never: The Remixes* hitting the top spot in February, and his duet-packed *Under The Mistletoe* hitting the shops – and topping the charts – in time for Christmas.

'Marketing experts at the label told us we could expect to move 60,000 in five weeks. We ended up selling 900,000 in five weeks.'

JUSTIN BIEBER ON *MY WORLD*'S SUCCESS

International Acclaim

If he carries on like this, pretty soon Justin will need an extra house to display all his awards, since his trophy cabinet must already be bulging under the weight of four American Music Awards won in 2010 and the six *Billboard* Music Awards he picked up in Las Vegas in May 2011.

He has also won a Brit, a CMT Award, two Canadian Juno Awards, four J-14 Teen Icon Awards, an MTV Brazil Award, three MTV Europe Awards, two MTV Video Music Awards, an MTV Movie Award, eight Teen Choice Awards, a Young Hollywood Award, a VH1 Award and a TRL Award – not to mention the scores of nominations he has had. The singer admitted he was disappointed after being snubbed by the People's Choice Awards, and he would probably rather forget the gongs he scooped for Least Stylish and Worst Album at the NME Awards in London in 2011. He was also devastated not to win at the prestigious Grammy Awards in January 2010, where he had been invited to present an award.

'I'm 17 ... every day is crazy to me because I see so many people and I get to make so many people smile.'

JUSTIN BIEBER

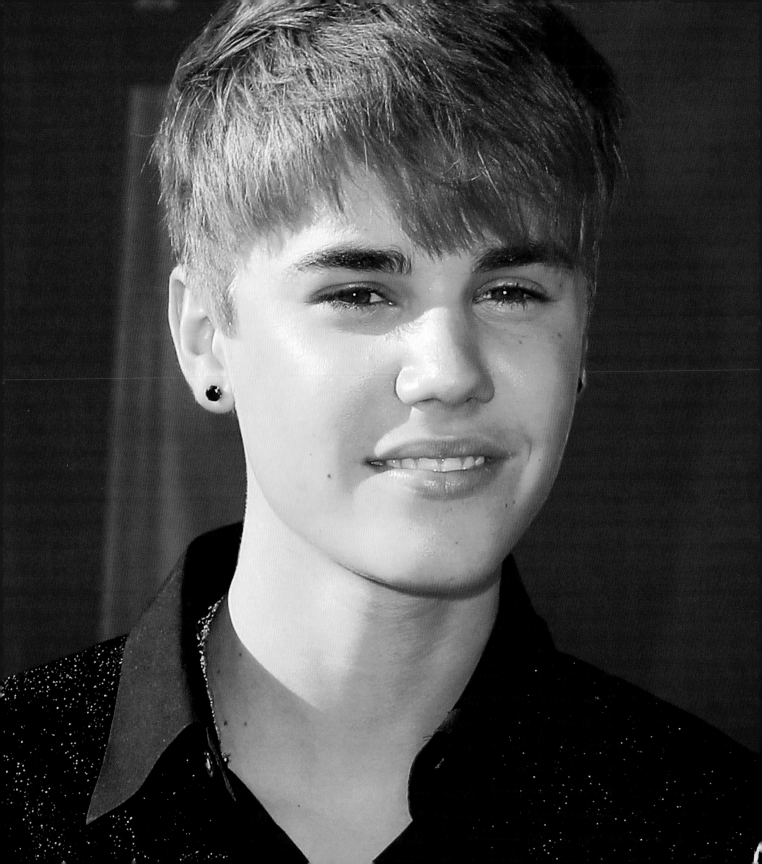

Money, Money, Money

We all know girls swoon at the sight and sound of JB, but having banked a staggering $100 million by the age of 17, he has been getting the moneymen's pulses racing too. These days he rakes in around £183,000 ($300,000) for each concert he performs, as well as cash from record sales, merchandising, personal appearances and celebrity endorsements. His phenomenal popularity means he is in huge demand for appearances in advertisements. He was paid £630,000 ($1 million) for donning a spacesuit and uttering a few words in a 30-second TV commercial for technology retail giant Best Buy, transmitted during the US Super Bowl in 2011, and his baby-faced good looks won him a £1.2 million ($1.9 million) contract to endorse the American acne treatment Proactiv.

Justin also supplements his income with a range of bed linen, headphones, scented children's jewellery, perfume and even a brand of nail varnish called One Less Lonely Girl. His 3-D movie *Justin Bieber: Never Say Never* helped to boost the coffers further (after just two weeks the film took $48 million – £29 million – in ticket sales in the US) and he earns even more cash from fans who collect Bieber dolls. Despite his vast wealth, Justin will not get his hands on the cash for a while; for now he is given an allowance of just £30 a day, which he considers sensible.

'My mom wants me to learn how to be very smart with my money. I grew up with not a lot of money. We never owned a house. I want to buy my mom a house.'

JUSTIN BIEBER

'My world got very big, very fast and, based on a lot of sad examples from the past, a lot of people expect me to get lost in it.'

JUSTIN BIEBER

Right Time, Right Face

With his super-cute looks and his distinctive side-swept hair flopping over his eyes, it is pretty easy to see why teenage girls sob with hysteria when Justin takes to the stage or why his concerts sell out in a matter of hours and fans queue for ages just to catch a glimpse of the biggest pop phenomenon of our generation. His clean-cut image and Christian beliefs made him a universal sensation (the hit TV show *Glee* dedicated an entire episode to him, and the Middleton's (parents of Kate) have even launched a range of Bieber merchandise through their event planning website Party Pieces). But his immense popularity often causes safety concerns.

The first time Justin visited London, in 2010, he was besieged with a frenzy of attention so intense that he was forced to appeal for calm on Twitter: 'Girls of London ... please don't bang on the windows of the car when we're moving,' he wrote. 'U can get hurt. No need for that. I got love for all of u :)'. He later said, 'Crowds and fans around London are insane.' However, his wholesome lifestyle, as well as his down-to-earth attitude to success, has won him an army of supporters.

Bieber Epidemic

Justin is constantly paying tribute to his fans on Twitter and during his live performances. His high-profile fans include a

three-year-old girl called Cody, who posted a video of herself crying because she could not see him, and a cancer sufferer called Sabrina Moreino, who has publicly credited Justin with helping her through the ordeal of chemotherapy. She wrote to him recalling a brief meeting, when he gave her his hat: 'Words can never express how much that one seemingly little gesture helped me overcome the terrible disease my body was fighting.' And Justin has confessed that he enjoys the attention of his besotted fans. 'There is no cure,' he admitted recently, 'for Bieber fever.'

'Every one of my fans is special to me. I love being in the studio but not as much as I love performing live because that's when I get to connect with you.'

JUSTIN BIEBER

'The success I've achieved comes to me from God, through the people who love and support me, and I include my fans in that.'

JUSTIN BIEBER

The Beliebers

Justin's rapid rise to fame even led to new expressions being coined: his fans are 'Beliebers' and the infectious nature of his popularity is 'Bieber fever'. But his die-hard fans have caused problems and appearances have been cancelled when the crowds spun out of control. Over 35 police units had to be called to a shopping mall in Long Island when Justin was scheduled to appear in March 2010. Justin's manager Scooter Braun was arrested for reckless endangerment and criminal nuisance, while a senior executive from Justin's label Island Records was also arrested for hindering crowd control efforts by not sending a timely message on Twitter as instructed by the police.

A month later Australian police cancelled another performance after girls were injured in a crush. Justin tweeted: 'I woke up this morning to the police canceling the show for safety reasons. I'm very happy about the welcome and the love from around the world, but I want everyone to still remember my fans' safety comes first. At the end of the day I want you all to enjoy the music.' In Liverpool in March 2011, on his day off before his concert, Justin was not allowed to step outside his hotel. Police warned that he could be arrested for 'inciting a riot' if he did. But Justin always takes time to thank the Beliebers for their support.

'Without Michael Jackson, none of us would be here.'

JUSTIN BIEBER

The New King of Pop?

As he collected an impressive four trophies at the American Music Awards in 2010, Justin paid tribute to one of his greatest heroes, saying, 'Music is music, and I'm definitely influenced by Michael Jackson and Boyz II Men and people who were black artists – that's what I like. But I like their voices and I like how they entertain – it's not about what colour they are. Michael was able to reach audiences from young to old; he never limited himself. He was so broad, everybody loved him, and that's what my goal is: to basically make people happy, to inspire them and to have everyone root for me.' Justin was devastated when Jackson died. He said later, 'One of my greatest idols, and my inspiration, was gone.'

And yet, the legendary music producer will.i.am, who has been working with Justin on his latest album, has predicted that the young star's career could prove to be as long as that of the former King of Pop. He explained, 'Justin Bieber could be like Prince. Justin Bieber could be like Michael Jackson where his career is like, "Wow, your career is so long. You're the first artist to be broadcast to Mars." Justin Bieber could be that dude.'

'I would **love** to **collaborate** with Beyoncé. She's beautiful.'

JUSTIN BIEBER

Bootylicious Beyoncé

Although Justin had always been a huge music lover, the first time he became a real fan was when he discovered Beyoncé and Destiny's Child, in 2001. At the 2010 Grammy Awards, where he was invited as a presenter, he admits to being starstruck when seeing her in the front row. He said, 'To my delight, sitting in the front row was my longtime crush, Beyoncé. She was so beautiful. Sorry, Jay-Z, I'm not trying to hit on your girl but I'm just saying.' Justin was so flustered by the sight of the singer that, when he was supposed to introduce Bon Jovi, he announced Beyoncé's name instead and stammered, 'Sorry, Beyoncé's always on my mind.' The 'Bootylicious' singer herself consoled him after the show, which appeared only to deepen his devotion: Justin admits that he still has a burning ambition to perform a duet with his ideal woman.

Big Players

Justin was only 13 when he first met R&B star Usher and he credits him with masterminding his career from the start. Usher was among the first to spot Justin's potential: as soon as he heard the young boy sing, he whisked him away for a meeting with producer LA Reid who immediately signed him to a lucrative record deal. Justin and Usher remain close friends and speak most days. Like Justin, Usher started out in singing competitions – his break was on a TV talent show called *Star Search* – which led to him being mentored by

Sean 'P. Diddy' Combs. The latter also takes a close interest in Justin's career and even gave him a white Lamborghini for his sixteenth birthday – the same day as Usher presented him with a Range Rover. Although he had the wheels and the glitzy friends, things did not quite work out as he expected. He failed his driving test the first time he attempted it and was so furious about missing out on his licence that he walked home in the rain rather than allow his mother to drive him. But when he is down like that, Usher is always around to offer advice or a shoulder to cry on. With 45 million record sales under his belt, Usher certainly knows what it takes to be a star in the cut-throat music industry and is a constant source of inspiration to Justin. The pair has a secret handshake and he often makes appearances on stage at Justin's shows.

'Usher says some songs work best when there's a sob in the singer's voice. You gotta let that deep feeling come through.'

JUSTIN BIEBER

Teenage Mom

Justin was born on 1 March 1994 in the town of Stratford in Ontario, Canada, where he was raised by his teenage mother, Patricia Lynn Mallette. Pattie, who struggled with drugs, alcohol and a suicide attempt before she gave birth to her son at 18, juggled several low-paid jobs to make ends meet and abandoned her dreams of becoming an actress. Justin said recently, 'I admire my mom so much for how she stepped up to meet all the challenges in her life. There were no luxuries at our little apartment, but it never occurred to me that we were poor. We had each other, which was everything we needed.'

He also added, 'My mom has been upfront and honest with me about the choices she made when she was my age, some of which were not the best and made life difficult for her and her family. After she had me, she had to work really hard all the time, but she never complained.'

It's A Family Thing

Although his parents split when he was just 10 months old, Justin has always maintained a close relationship with his dad Jeremy, who went on to marry another woman and have two children. While Pattie worked, her French-speaking parents stepped in to help care for Justin – he had his own bedroom at their house – and as a result he is still very close to his grandparents. He said, 'My life is working out pretty sweet and

'I admire her [Justin's mother] so much for how she learned from her mistakes, got her life together and made a life for me.'

JUSTIN BIEBER

every morning I wake up grateful for the blessings that I have.' Proud Pattie still travels with Justin and ensures he keeps his feet on the ground despite all the adulation and global stardom coming his way. He has a curfew and she confiscates his phone or laptop if he misbehaves or breaks the rules, which include getting eight hours' sleep a night, maintaining good grades and being polite. Justin recently said that they're just like every other teenager and their mum. 'We argue, yes, I think every parent and son argue, but I love my mom,' he said. 'I think it's good she travels with me, but sometimes I need a break because I'm with her 24/7 but I love her.'

'It sucked for my mom because being a single parent is never easy, especially with a little prankster like me.' JUSTIN BIEBER

Doing It His Way

Anyone who dismisses Justin as little more than a pretty face with a sweet voice needs to think again. The schoolboy's talent was obvious even long before he conquered the pop world. Justin started drumming when he was just two years old. 'Back in 1996, Mom says I was all about the beat. I'd wail

'I could feel it when the chords and melody didn't fit together, the same way you can feel it when your shoes are on the wrong feet.'

JUSTIN BIEBER

on whatever was handy – pots and pans, plastic bowls, tables and chairs. I was basically banging on everything I could get my hands on,' he says.

Although the church held a benefit to help Pattie pay for a drum kit, money was tight so Justin taught himself to play the guitar, piano, trumpet and drums, even though he could not read music. Pattie took Justin along every Sunday to the church band she had joined, where his talents were first noticed. Although Justin was also keen on hockey, football and chess, by the time he reached his teens his self-taught ability had become quite remarkable and, with the help of natural rhythm, he developed into a multi-talented musician. Pretty impressive, right?

This Is It!

In early 2007, when he was just 12 years old and too young to enter *American Idol*, Justin paid $2 to enter a local singing contest in his hometown. Although he was the only entrant who had not been taking singing lessons and without a vocal coach, he won third place singing Aretha Franklin's hit 'Respect'. He said, 'This was the first time I heard an audience actually cheer for me on stage and it felt pretty good. Girls were screaming for me.' Pattie posted a video of the performance on the YouTube website, telling her son, 'I wish everyone could have been there – the whole family and friends at church. But I got some great videos. I'm going to put them up on YouTube so everyone can see how amazing you did.' That decision was to change Justin's life for ever.

'Disney World plus girls. Busking was a pretty sweet gig!'

JUSTIN BIEBER

Busking Around

The same summer as he entered the singing competition, Justin learnt his early performance skills by busking on the streets. He did not have enough money to play golf with his friends, so he opened his guitar case and started busking in front of a Stratford theatre during the annual Shakespeare Festival, when the town is teeming with tourists. He made $200 in his first two hours and earned nearly $3,000 in total, which was enough to take his family to Disney World – their first ever holiday. He recalled. 'I felt like I'd discovered a gold mine. People were very kind and supportive.' As well as throwing cash into his open guitar case, girls would leave notes with their phone numbers and Justin could not believe his luck. There is now a star plaque on the spot where Justin used to stand.

Home Movies

Pattie's film clips quickly developed a following on YouTube, so she continued to upload dozens more of her soulful boy singing Christian songs and covers of various R&B songs by artists including Stevie Wonder and Usher. Tourists who watched Justin busking added their videos too, and his popularity rapidly grew. By the end of that summer one video had been viewed 72,000 times, and Pattie started receiving calls from people offering to manage Justin.

The home videos showcasing Justin's charisma and natural energy attracted millions of viewers and Justin could not believe his luck when he realized; 'It turned out that other people liked them and they started subscribing to them,' he said.

By chance, Scooter had seen a performance of Justin sitting on a couch, strumming his guitar and singing like an angel. The film, shot by his mother and posted on the web by his grandmother Kate, became a sensation. Scooter thought he had found the next Michael Jackson. Once Scooter had signed him to a lucrative record deal, they decided to continue posting clips on YouTube. Thanks to Justin's massive online following (that now runs into millions), Scooter felt it was an effective way to reach his fans, and so together they started to produce slicker videos for the site. Justin has commented that, 'It was really cool going from my webcam to professional videos.' In July 2010, his single 'Baby', featuring Ludacris, clocked up more than 500 million hits, making it the most watched video in YouTube's history.

'That's how my manager found me. He saw me on YouTube and contacted my family and now I'm signed!' JUSTIN BIEBER

'He [Scooter Braun] was

very, very persistent.

He even called my

great-aunt and my

school board.'

JUSTIN BIEBER

A Record Deal

Once Scooter had spotted the young singer's potential, he would stop at nothing to land him a lucrative record deal. At first Pattie was suspicious of Scooter's motives, but eventually she let him talk to Justin, who recalled, 'After an hour or so, we were talking as if we'd known each other for years. We really are a lot alike in many ways, one of the most important being that we like the same music.' In autumn 2007, Scooter flew Justin and Pattie to Atlanta. Justin admits he was overwhelmed – it was the first time he had ever been on a plane – but one of the first people he met was his hero Usher, in the car park of his recording studio! Ambitious Justin immediately offered to sing but Usher turned him down, saying, 'Nah, little buddy, it's cold out here.'

It would be another year before Justin met Usher again, and Justin still teases his mentor about brushing him off that first day. Scooter reassured Pattie by introducing them to his close-knit family and promising to plan Justin's career carefully. They agreed to continue to post videos on YouTube in order to accumulate a fanbase. All his clips got a million hits, almost immediately, and Justin's trips to Atlanta became more and more frequent. Suddenly, Usher and pop superstar Justin Timberlake were fighting over Justin, as both were eager to mentor the young singer. Eventually, Usher won and said later, 'He was an amazing talent and find. Given my experience, I knew exactly what it would take for him to become an incredible artist.' Justin quickly signed with Island Records and RBMG, and never looked back, although he continues to upload videos on to YouTube to help create buzz around new releases.

Movers & Skaters

Scooter was born in New York in 1981 and is one of the most powerful players in the music business, thanks to his discovery of Justin in 2007. He said, 'He is the son I didn't have. If he has done something wrong, he has to apologize. Justin isn't treated with kid gloves. I've sacked people who have pandered to him. He's a kid. He's not perfect. You have to set boundaries.'

Although Pattie had her reservations about Scooter when he first appeared on the scene, she praised him during a recent appearance on *The Oprah Winfrey Show* for keeping her son grounded. In turn, Scooter Braun credits Pattie with keeping Justin out of trouble and commented, 'I think his mother feels that if they were still in Stratford, Ontario, he'd be getting himself into a lot of trouble. Justin doesn't study the people who made it. He studies the people who haven't.' Justin himself says he is grateful for Scooter's guidance: 'I'm surrounded by super-smart, super-talented, extremely good people who love me and watch out for me every step of the way. They don't let me lose sight of where I came from or where I'm going.'

Although it was Scooter who introduced Justin to legendary producer LA Reid, who then signed him to Island Def Jam Records, at the time all Justin wanted to know was whether his tour bus would be fitted with an Xbox!

Ushering in Usher

When global superstar Usher struck a money-spinning business deal with Justin in 2008, the fledgling singer had an impressive internet following, but he was yet to become the phenomenon we see today. They met when Scooter flew Justin to Usher's hometown of Atlanta, Georgia, and although he turned down Justin's first offer to sing for him, Usher instinctively knew he was in the presence of a precocious talent, not unlike his younger self, and a year later Justin finally sang for him. Usher was impressed: 'I thought, OK, if this [Justin's talent] is properly nourished it could become huge. But I didn't know how huge.' Since then the R&B star with 45 million record sales to his name has taken Justin under his wing, nurtured his talent and helped Scooter orchestrate his rapid rise to fame. Usher told him, 'All of my experiences I want to share, all my knowledge. I want to share it with you and help you make this moment happen.'

'The day I met Justin was special. I saw that he had a raw talent and he was cute; girls would like him.'

USHER

'He's got **Scooter**, and the **team** around **us** is there to **protect** his character and treat him like a **kid**, and to make sure he has **fun** and **stays grounded**.'

PATTIE MALLETTE

Starstruck

A former child star himself, Mr Timberlake was also keen to mentor Mr B in the early days and flew him to his Memphis home, where Justin met his girlfriend at the time, Jessica Biel, and performed 'Cry Me A River'. Timberlake recalled later, 'It takes a lot of balls to sing me my own song.' They hung out together, watching basketball, and became friends. 'Timberlake is someone to this day I look up to and study his career,' said Justin. 'It was so surreal that he wanted to do a deal with me, just a kid from a small town in Canada.'

Although Timberlake lost out to Usher, he has continued to keep a close eye on Justin's career. 'I just hope he has a good support system because it's awkward growing up in front of the public,' he said. 'Justin's probably dealing with that on some level now. You need to have a plan, and somebody like Justin Bieber should be thinking about that right now. Otherwise, before you know it, there's going to be some kid who's younger than you. We just live in that age.'

'It was a **weird feeling**. The video ['One Time'] stayed in the **Top 10** with all those **amazing videos** by Michael, **one** of the **great artists** of all **time**.'

JUSTIN BIEBER

First Time

After moving with Pattie from Stratford to Atlanta, Justin finally got into a recording studio. 'I've never worked so hard in my life,' he said. And his first single 'One Time', released in July 2009, was an immediate hit, smashing the charts around the world and going platinum in America, Canada and Australia, and reaching the Top 20 in Britain, Germany, France and New Zealand. Taken from his debut album *My World* and produced by Tricky, the video features Justin's mentor Usher asking him to look after his house, but Justin ends up throwing a wild pool party with his old school friend Ryan Butler. By the end of the video, Justin is left disappointed when the girl he was singing to, played by Kristen Rodeheaver, kisses him on the cheek and then leaves. He tries to chase after her but gets caught by Usher. His first ever tweet urged people to check out 'One Time' on Myspace, and two days later it was the No. 3 video on iTunes. 'It was mind-blowing; we'd made it. We'd proved we could do it.' But 'One Time' was kept off the top spot by the death of Michael Jackson whose songs were re-released following the tragedy.

While performing the song on tour in London in 2009, he fractured his foot but carried on until the end of the tune, to the delight of his ardent admirers. By January 2010, the video had been viewed over 100 million times on the internet – and it is the fifth most viewed video in YouTube history.

'It's kind of **hard** to **balance school work** sometimes. But **at** times, like, if I'm going to **the White House** and **I'm** here doing **a tour** and **stuff**, that's like **school**.'

JUSTIN BIEBER

'One Less Lonely Girl'

Justin's second single was released exclusively on iTunes in October 2009 and immediately flew into the Top 10 in Canada and Top 15 in the United States, before charting high around the world. Within weeks, two more singles were released on iTunes – 'Love Me' and 'Favorite Girl' – and both were huge hits, leading to his tour tickets selling out in minutes. He revealed his songwriting is inspired by real events in his life and that he wrote 'Down To Earth' about his parents' separation. Following his three hits in rapid succession, Justin admitted it was difficult to keep his feet on the ground when he was being pulled in so many different directions.

My World

Justin's debut album was produced by LA Reid and released in two parts, with *My World* hitting the charts in November 2009. Produced by Usher, the highly acclaimed R&B-style songs were inspired mostly by teen romance and the album was backed up by a huge promotional tour, with Justin appearing on radio and TV shows all over America. 'We sat in airports for hours, jamming and writing songs between flights,' Justin recalled. 'We did interviews day after day, hearing the same jokes about my hair and my size and my age.'

In the States it sold 137,000 copies in its first week and 900,000 in five weeks. It entered the Canadian charts at No. 1, certified double platinum within a month.

Following 'One Time', the next three singles – 'One Less Lonely Girl', 'Love Me' and 'Favorite Girl' – were released exclusively on iTunes. To support the album, he embarked on a promotional blitz, which included his first major tour.

'Everything about the way My World was released turned the old way of thinking inside out. A skinny white kid on a record with rappers with serious street cred. A teen fan favorite with no TV show.'

JUSTIN BIEBER

Out of This World

The second part of Justin's studio album, released in March 2010, was always destined to be a hit thanks to the huge level of anticipation that was built up before he had even started work on it. Fans were desperate for more songs from Justin and, when it came out, critics were kind. They proclaimed it more mature than the first release, with an edgier hip-hop sound. Justin, who had been afraid of being dismissed as little more than a teen pin-up, was delighted that the music industry seemed to be taking him seriously.

Of course, *My World 2.0* debuted at No. 1 in the States, selling 283,000 copies in its first week; this meant that Justin became the youngest solo male artist to top the chart since Stevie Wonder, in 1963, and the first act since The Beatles to debut at No. 1 and then sell more the following week. The album also peaked at No. 1 in Canada, Ireland, Spain, Australia and New Zealand.

'I **wanted** to do **something** that was a little bit **more R&B** and that could **reach out** to everyone. I **just** wanted to be **able** to show my **vocal abilities**.' JUSTIN BIEBER

'Baby'

Justin's mega-hit single features the rapper Ludacris, who is now a close friend. Although at first glance they might seem like an odd match, they are seen bowling together in the video, which became the most viewed piece of footage on YouTube ever, racking up more than 459 million hits in the months following its release in February 2010. Those closest to Justin were worried the global fame would go to his head and could lead to him going off the rails like so many other young stars before him, but Justin showed his sensible side by studying the devastating effect huge stardom had on his hero Michael Jackson.

'Michael was very serious about his craft. He'd say don't get caught up in whatever that moment is, be mindful that you're always ... making history. It inspired me to come up with my mantra: what we do in this lifetime echoes through eternity.' JUSTIN BIEBER

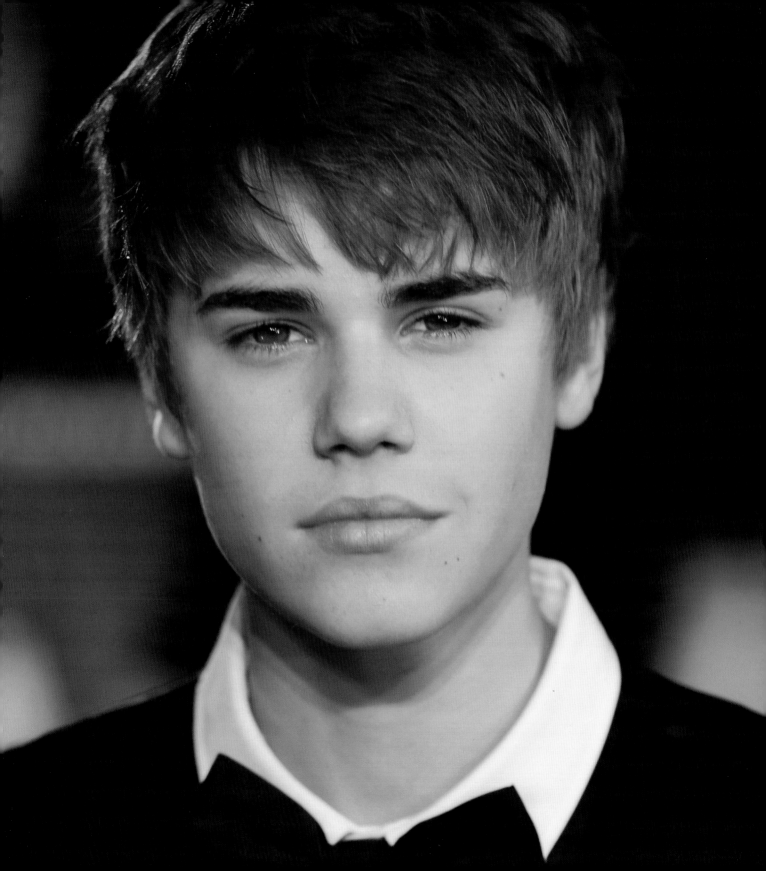

'To see the No. 1 song goes to help Haiti is awesome. Would rather that be No. 1 and help the people in need.'

JUSTIN BIEBER (ON TWITTER)

Doing His Bit

Justin teamed up with a host of the biggest names in music to raise money for Haiti by recording 'We Are The World', which was originally released by Michael Jackson in 1985 to raise funds for the famine in Africa. Along with stars including Lady Gaga and Miley Cyrus, he recorded the song in January 2010 to benefit victims of the earthquake. He scored one of the few solos: the opening verse which had been originally sung by Lionel Ritchie. But he said it was hard to concentrate in front of former Pussycat Dolls singer Nicole Scherzinger. 'It was hard for me to take my eyes off of her because she's so gorgeous,' Justin said. Justin also performed a medley of his hits at the *SOS: Help For Haiti* a month later, changing the chorus of 'Baby' to 'Baby, baby, Haiti.'

He's Got The Look

There is no denying it: Justin's image is really all about the hair and that famous side-swept style – known simply as The Bieber – which quickly became the most requested look of teenage boys around the globe. Of course, the fresh-faced good looks and the lithe body did no harm, but the hair was making headlines all by itself! *The New York Times* reported that salons were charging almost £100 to recreate the same hairstyle for boys hoping to match Justin's success with girls. Although some boys were too embarrassed to ask for it by name, The Bieber was soon everywhere, and the singer was even persuaded to reveal his styling secrets in MTV's *The Diary of Justin Bieber*. In the much-watched (and much-copied) episode, Justin was seen using a combination of towel drying and blow-drying to achieve hair perfection quickly and expertly – without the aid of a professional stylist!

In February 2011, when he finally changed his style for what he described as 'kind of a mature look', the event was reported around the world and the hair that was taken was collected and sold for charity, raising over $40,000 in an auction.

Dressed To Impress

Most fans would argue that Justin always looked good, dressed simply in jeans and his beloved purple hoodies, but shortly before he embarked on his first promotional tour,

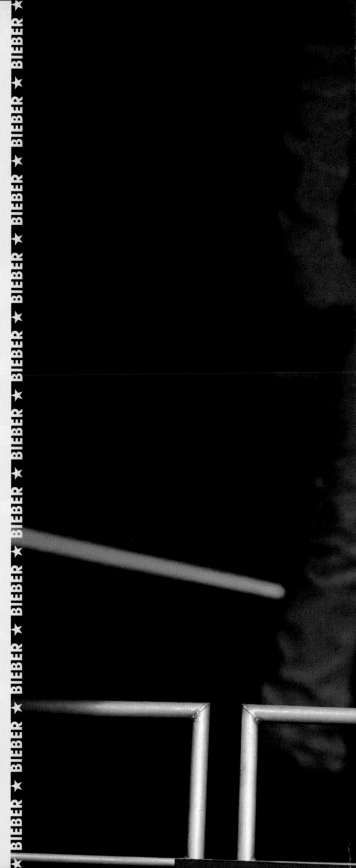

following the release of 'One Time' in 2009, Usher hired a stylist called Ryan Good to make sure the young star looked as sharp and fresh as possible. Justin said, 'Style can be how you carry yourself and how you wear whatever you have on. I like to consider my style as very relatable. Usually, I'm in blue jeans and a hoody, and the rest is my attitude. I don't know if it's possible to style another person but Ry keeps my head on straight so I don't come off like a douche bag. Mostly, he's a friend who's honest with me. Everyone should have at least one of those, and I'm fortunate to have several.'

Luckily, his devoted Beliebers are always thrilled by his outfits and do not even seem to mind that he is only 1.65 m (5 ft 5 in) tall. Since he is still growing, Justin is not concerned either.

'I don't think it's the hair, he's got game, he knows what he's doing ... He's a very sweet kid and he loves his fans.'

SELENA GOMEZ

'I put in a lot of time on the road going to radio stations at 6 a.m. and singing, all in the middle of my growth spurt. Thanks to the music industry, I'm going to be really short.'

JUSTIN BIEBER

'... Five minutes ... like, seriously. People are always like, "Yeah, right." I get out of the shower, I blow-dry it and then it's done in, like, five minutes.'

JUSTIN BIEBER

Mini-me

Not many celebs receive the honour of having a Madame Tussauds waxwork made before they even reach their eighteenth birthday, but Justin was thrilled to bits when the London museum unveiled his lookalike in March 2011, alongside world leaders and Hollywood A-listers. When he visited London to see the model for himself, Justin declared it to be 'awesome', adding, 'It's pretty incredible to see. I'm taller but this was a point in time.' Stylists from the museum teamed up with Bieber's personal hair stylist to ensure his once legendary hairstyle was the exact replica of the original cut; however, two weeks before the model was unveiled, Justin changed his style to a shorter, more textured cut – much to the dismay of his fans.

As well as the waxwork, there are plenty of other ways for fans to get up close and personal with the man of the moment. Toy shops are now selling out of a range of three lifelike Justin dolls wearing different outfits, as well as a separate range of JB dolls which boast the signature swoop haircut that fans can style themselves – and The Real Hairstyle dolls even sing a selection of his biggest hits!

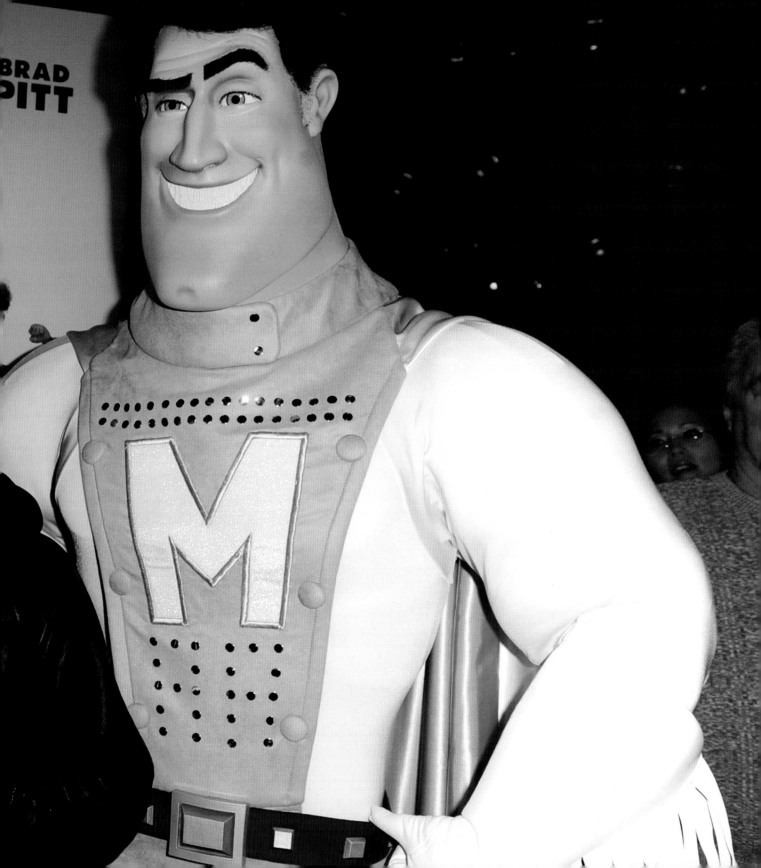

The Bieber Machine

Justin admits that the toughest time is when he takes his show on the road. He says, 'A lot of hard work goes into performing. My set is 75 minutes long and it's not easy. I work hard on endurance training. There are more than 500 people working to make sure the show goes perfect.' His entourage now includes stylist Ryan Good, vocal coach Jan Smith, choreographer Jamaica Craft, Scooter's girlfriend Carin, bodyguard Kenny Hamilton and his tutor Jenny who works for the School of Young Performers which specializes in educating children in the entertainment industry.

Justin's recent gruelling worldwide 140-date tour, which saw him travel the globe from Manchester to Melbourne, was an instant sellout, raking in $600,000 a night. After his single 'One Time' reached the Top 20 in five countries, he needed a global promotional spree so his My World Tour kicked off in June 2010. Despite performing to huge crowds at 85 shows in six months, Justin says he never suffers from nerves or stage fright. 'I don't mean for that to come off as cocky,' he says. 'I just don't see what's to be afraid of. It's not that I never make mistakes, but that's life. You pick it up and keep going.' A dollar of every ticket sold goes to Pencils of Promise, a charity that builds schools in developing world countries. So far his contributions have led to 50 new schools.

'Michael Jackson was the most giving artist of all time. If I can do just one-tenth of the good he did for others, I can really make a difference in this world.'

JUSTIN BIEBER

Unstoppable On The Road

When he first hit the big time, Justin was so busy working on his first studio recordings that he was not fully aware of how popular he had become, until the notorious riot in a Long Island mall, which ended with Scooter's arrest. The rest of 2009 was a whirlwind for Justin as he crisscrossed the globe appearing on German TV shows, at Japanese record stores, singing to his Parisian fans in French and even bungee jumping in New Zealand. He performed to a crowd of 12,000 Beliebers at Wembley Arena when he opened a show for Taylor Swift, but later admitted that all the travel took its toll: 'I know this all sounds like fun,' he said. 'But there was plenty of times I was so exhausted I felt like I was losing myself.' It was during the Wembley show that Justin slipped off a ramp on the stage and broke his foot in the middle of a song, but even that did not stop him giving the fans what they wanted. 'I kept singing, and the crowd kept going crazy, but people onstage were looking at me like they knew something was wrong. All I could do was fight for enough air to get through the song.'

'It was crazy. Media reports kept comparing it to Beatlemania. Suddenly, the whole world was paying attention.' JUSTIN BIEBER

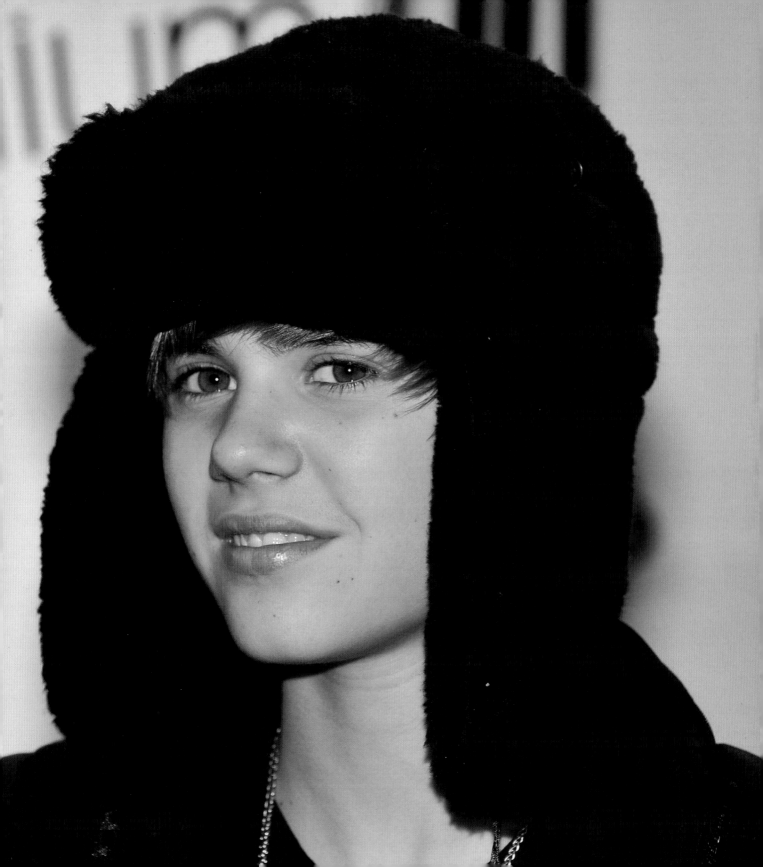

White House Songbird

Justin had become a sensation on YouTube but it was only really when he was invited to sing for the US President Barack Obama at the White House in December 2009 that he felt he had been propelled to mainstream stardom, and the world really started to take notice. Joined by his mentor Usher and Mary J. Blige, Justin performed at the Christmas in Washington concert, which he admitted was a nerve-wracking experience. Although he had a broken foot at the time, Justin impressed the First Family and their guests with his rendition of Stevie Wonder's 'Someday at Christmas', and from that moment life changed for ever for Justin – he had to leave school and hire a private tutor.

He and Pattie packed up and moved from Stratford to Atlanta, and he has been on the road almost constantly since then. 'A year later,' said Pattie when asked about posting the YouTube videos, 'the baby I diapered has played Madison Square Garden and sung for the president of the United States. It's crazy.'

'I'm nervous. If I mess up, he [Barack Obama] might deport me back to Canada. Lol.'

JUSTIN BIEBER (ON TWITTER)

A YouTube Star Is Born

As soon as Usher heard about the way Justin had promoted himself via YouTube, he was blown away because it was so different from the way other young stars find fame. He recalled, 'I knew if we could guide him then we'd have a product that is the Justin you see.' Justin's very first clip – of him covering a Ne-Yo song – went viral and scored a million hits within weeks, and to date the music video for Bieber's hit song 'Baby' has been viewed on YouTube a record 500 million times (the first 10 million were purely through word of mouth). He is the first real YouTube sensation to cross over to the mainstream and the site, which allows anyone to post film clips, is the reason for much of his appeal. Of course, many people have tried to imitate Justin's success; indeed, a female folk singer called Dani Shay, who bears a striking resemblance to Justin, also became a sensation on the site when she posted a video of herself singing 'Baby', which was immediately viewed by a staggering 230,000 people.

Loving The Tweets

'Don't believe dreams come true? Think about this: I'm following more people on Twitter than live in my entire hometown,' Justin tweeted in April 2011 from his Twitter account, which has been consistently gaining followers at an

'At that time, there was a pop phenomenon that was all very Disney and Nickelodeon. But here was a guy who was the antithesis to all that. He had introduced himself to the world online.'

USHER

'I'm 15 y/o, a simple girl who simply love @justinbieber and a BELIEBER ... my dream is to be followed by Justin Bieber someday.'

A BIEBER FAN'S TWITTER PROFILE

average of 24,000 per day. Statistics change daily, but he is usually the second most followed person on Twitter, after Lady Gaga. He has more followers than Barack Obama, who is generally third. He is constantly keeping his fans informed and entertained with his regular tweets, which are often trending on the site, although he caused chaos when he pretended to post his own phone number – urging fans to call him – but in fact gave the number of an old enemy, who was bombarded with thousands of calls and 26,000 text messages.

Justin's followers follow each other, and they follow whoever he follows. And they routinely tweet him pleas to follow them, longing for the day he will finally do that. If he does follow them, they memorialize the date on their profiles ('JB followed me 11/02/09!!'). According to a report published in the *Observer* newspaper, Justin has become more influential in the social networking sphere than Barack Obama or even the Dalai Lama.

Well Liked

Justin's phenomenal fanbase on Facebook – he currently has well over 37 million followers – has also helped him be named as the third most powerful entertainer in the world. A social networking index called Klout, which adds up a person's tweets, updates and Google mentions, ranked Justin Bieber as the most influential person in cyberspace.

Justin uses Facebook to promote tour dates and upcoming releases, which are immediately shared by fans who are always on the lookout for updates. Although the social networking site is also full of pages criticizing the young Canadian star (the I Hate Justin Bieber Club has well over 50,000 followers) and his vast earnings, he claims to be unfazed by all of it and remains positive about his fame. With his daily allowance and strict rules, his manager Scooter makes sure he does not spend every spare minute looking at a screen. If Justin misbehaves the first

things to be confiscated are his laptop and phone to stop him posting updates and interacting with his friends and fans online.

'We have rules to keep him in line. We treat him like any other teenager.' SCOOTER BRAUN

'There's more people that like me than there are who hate me, so I kind of brush it off.'

JUSTIN BIEBER

Justin In Print

Justin has made it on to the cover of almost every magazine, from *OK!* to the controversial *Rolling Stone* interview when he said he 'really doesn't believe in abortion'. Of course, there are regular publications devoted entirely to him and special collector's issues of teen magazines revealing all kinds of details such as the name of his dog (Sam!) and his favourite colour (purple!).

But insiders say his huge popularity does not necessarily carry over to the newsstands. When he appeared on the cover of *Vanity Fair* in February 2011, covered in lipstick kisses, it became the worst selling issue in 12 years (only 246,000 copies were sold, compared to the usual 500,000). Justin also meant bad news for other magazines including *Teen Vogue*, which saw sales drop by 12 per cent when he was on the cover in October 2010, and *People* magazine, which had its third worst ever seller when he was featured on the front in April 2010.

Media experts suggest that his fans do not need to buy magazines because they have regular contact with the star himself thanks to his daily Twitter updates.

From The Small Screen ...

Although he does not have a show of his own – yet – Justin has appeared on almost every major television programme across the globe. In the States he has been on *Piers Morgan*

Tonight twice, as well as appearing on *Glee*, *Conan*, *Live with Regis and Kelly*, *The Daily Show*, *Punk'd*, *The Barbara Walters Special*, *So You Think You Can Dance*, *Sunrise*, *Saturday Night Live*, *Late Night with Jimmy Fallon*, *The Tonight Show with Jay Leno*, *American Idol*, *The Late Show with David Letterman*, *The View*, *Entertainment Tonight*, *Ellen*, *Today* … The list goes on.

Here in the UK he has appeared on *The Graham Norton Show*, *The X-Factor*, *Alan Carr: Chatty Man*, *Let's Dance For Sport Relief*, *GMTV* and *It's On With Alexa Chung*. He has also popped up on shows across Europe and Japan, where he has become a major star. Justin was expected to make a series of appearances on British TV at the end of 2011, including a special performance of some of his biggest hits on *The X-Factor*.

'That's my hair. I'm giving pieces of it to different people.'"

JUSTIN BIEBER AFTER PRESENTING CHAT

SHOW HOST ELLEN DEGENERES WITH A

LOCK OF HIS HAIR IN A GLASS BOX

... To The Big Screen

Justin's fans can look forward to seeing a lot more of their pin-up as he makes the inevitable move into acting. He starred in his own hugely successful movie *Never Say Never*, which grossed $72 million worldwide. The film followed his 2010 concert tour and featured appearances by Usher, Miley Cyrus, Boyz II Men, Sean Kingston and Jaden Smith.

He has already made a cameo appearance on the American drama *CSI* and won praise for his role as a member of an anti-government family whose foster dad is in jail and whose brother is out for revenge against the police. Afterwards, however, he was labelled a 'brat' by one of the show's leading stars, Marg Helgenberger, who commented, 'I shouldn't be saying this but he was kind of a brat. He locked one of the producers in a closet and he put his fist through a cake that was on the cast's table.'

Justin The Hologram

Next, Justin is to star alongside Ashton Kutcher in a big-budget movie called *What Would Kenny Do*, set to be released in 2013. Produced by Will Smith, it is a buddy comedy about a 17-year-old boy guided through high school by a hologram of himself as an adult.

Justin is also in talks with Hollywood hotshot Mark Wahlberg about a basketball movie. 'I've hung out with him enough and talked to him enough to know that I think we could make it real,' Mark said.

'It's something that would be very surprising to people, the kind of role that he would play, and what he would be capable of doing as an actor. It's more like Paul Newman and The Hustler.'

MARK WAHLBERG

Playing
Happy Families

Justin is often spotted with Selena Gomez (are-they-aren't-they?) holding hands and kissing. The couple hit the headlines when they posed in a series of photos as a family, in the style of Brad Pitt and Angelina Jolie's famous shoot which caused controversy when they first got together. At the time, Brad's ex-wife Jennifer Aniston accused him of 'missing a sensitivity chip', just as Justin's recreation of the 1950s-style image devastated his army of fans who realized how serious his romance with Selena had become. He tweeted the picture with the caption 'Brangelina 2.0'.

Even though he broke millions of hearts, Justin believes he is a good boyfriend. 'Scooter gave me the smartest dating advice you could ever give – to a guy or a girl – just listen. And that means really listen to what the other person is saying instead of using that time to come up with your next clever remark,' he said. 'I had a great advantage in that I lived in girl world all my life. My mom and I had talked about stuff pretty openly…'

Shockingly, after photos emerged of Justin and Selena kissing in Hawaii in the summer of 2011, she received thousands of threats from jealous fans. 'Stay away from Justin, pedophile,' one angry fan wrote on Twitter. Another sent the message: 'Selena Gomez is dangerously close to a long, slow painful death.' And on Facebook a page called 'I hate Selena Gomez cuz she is dating my man' attracted almost 2,000 people who

'… maybe I understood more than the average guy about how girls work. I wasn't afraid to talk to girls, hang out with girls, look at girls and flirt with girls.'

JUSTIN BIEBER

'He's the **one** who got me into **classic rock** and then **turned me** on to stuff like **Guns N' Roses** and **Metallica**. He taught me how to **drive** too. He's **cool**.'

JUSTIN BIEBER ON HIS FATHER

posted a series of derogatory comments. One fan warned, 'If Selena Gomez breaks Justin Bieber's heart, I will break her face; I will kill her without kindness.'

Father'n'Son

Although his dad Jeremy left when Justin was just 10 months old and went on to start a new family, they remain close, and Jeremy now often joins his son on tour. Justin wrote the song 'Where Are You Now' about his father. 'That song is about my dad and having him not always being there. But my dad and I now have a great relationship. And I'm fine that stuff like that is coming out. I want to sing about things that are going on in my life, and a lot of people will be able to relate to it.' Although it was originally his mother who helped him find fame, Justin credits his dad with introducing him to music. 'When I was younger, he taught me how to play some songs on the guitar, like "Knockin' on Heaven's Door" by Bob Dylan,' he explained.

Spiritual Side

Justin has been a devout Christian and regular churchgoer all his life; he prays before his performances and often speaks of his devotion to Jesus. He said recently, 'I like when people ask me about my religion because I love God, and I don't want to miss an opportunity to share that. I pray before every show and am thankful for every blessing.' Pattie, a born-again Christian, has also shared her strong religious beliefs on a

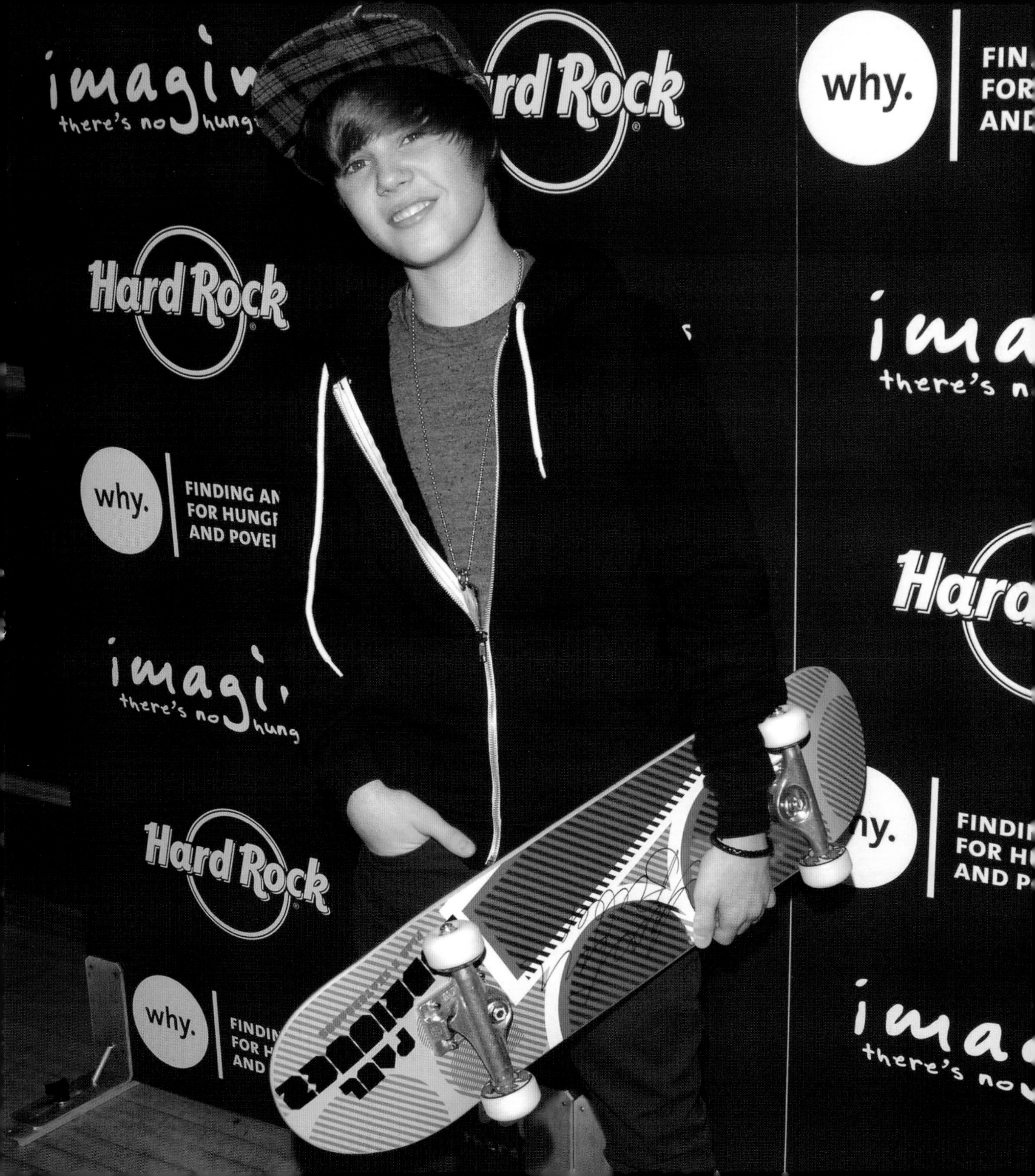

spiritual TV show, while Justin and his entourage always huddle together before a performance. During the huddles, Pattie thanks God for all their blessings, vocal coach Jan prays that Justin's voice will be empowered with love, while Justin prays for the safety of his dance crew and everyone backstage. His guitarist Dan Kanter then leads them all in an ancient Hebrew prayer giving thanks to God. Justin once revealed he often suffers from insomnia because he cannot stop thinking about important matters.

'I think about all the things I didn't have time to think about during the day – like family and God and things that should be more important.'

JUSTIN BIEBER

Myths

It was rumoured that Justin had struck up a close friendship with David Beckham after the pair were photographed next to each other at an LA Lakers basketball game in 2010, and the Beckhams continued the joke when Victoria tweeted a photo of David sunbathing next to a cardboard cutout of Justin. But, despite the Beckhams' kids being big fans, they are not friends. And despite his alleged friendships with other famous folk including Will Smith's son, Jayden, and the singer Taylor Swift, Justin is still closest to his oldest friends from Jeanne Sauvé Catholic School – Chaz Somers and Ryan Butler – who often join him on tour and have even appeared in his videos.

Another myth is that Justin is actually bald! There was widespread panic when fans thought Justin had lost his hair, but his appearance in a bald cap on the *Jimmy Kimmel Live* chat show in the US was just another of Justin's pranks. 'Fans can just focus on my beautiful, silky smooth vocals now,' he joked.

The Dark Side

Justin's huge popularity among pre-teen and teenage girls – including, of course, the devoted Beliebers – has occasionally led them to harshly criticize other women who

> 'Roses are red, violets are blue, @selenagomez if you'll break @justinbieber's heart I'm gonna kill you.'
>
> BIEBER FAN ON TWITTER

have been romantically linked with Justin. Any girl appearing to be close to Justin has received personal attacks, death threats and slanderous remarks – most notably, the socialite, entrepreneur and reality television star Kim Kardashian, singer Jasmine Villegas and Selena Gomez. One message read [see left]:

Justin also ran into trouble when his perfume Someday was launched, in a distinctive bottle which bore similarities to Marc Jacobs's fragrance, Lola. The designer said he considered suing Justin but eventually decided against it. Nevertheless, Justin's fruity fragrance proved a hit when he announced, 'Let's be real, the way a girl smells is very important to a guy!'

Justin has also had to face harsh critics who suggest his career will not last once he reaches adulthood. A recent poll by the website SodaHead showed that 76 per cent of teenage girls do not expect Justin's career to last and predicted that he would not be in the charts by 2021. 'Bieber's biggest roadblock is his lack of notable songs,' they claimed.

The Future

Justin has admitted he has plans to break millions of hearts by settling down with the future Mrs Bieber within the next few years.

Justin also seems to be spending an increasing amount of his time having to deny claims that he is badly behaved; he was allegedly rude to staff in a Starbucks at Las Vegas airport and then was forced to reject reports that he 'acted like a brat' on an American Airlines flight in August when he allegedly refused to take his seat during the preparations for takeoff and would not give the pilot an autograph.

Although he already boasts a bulging bank account and an army of devoted fans, Justin is showing no signs of slowing down. He is on track to become one of the most successful artists of all time, as well as one of the most generous: his album of high-profile duets, *Under The Mistletoe*, raised over $10m for charities, including Pencils of Promise and Make-A-Wish Foundation. Music industry experts predict Justin will be a huge star for years to come, and Justin is determined to prove his critics wrong: 'Doubt us … I like it that way,' he wrote on his Twitter account. 'Makes us work harder…just makes us want to prove you wrong. Every step we've been doubted. Why change now.'

'I definitely want to do more acting and further my career in that area; that's something I would love to do.' JUSTIN BIEBER

'I want to be a young dad. By 25 or 26 I want to see myself, like, married or start looking for a family.' JUSTIN BIEBER

Further Information

Justin Bieber Vital Info

Birth Name   Justin Drew Bieber

Birth Date   1 March 1994

Birth Place   London, Ontario, Canada

Height   1.65 m (5 ft 5 in)

Nationality   Canadian

Alter Egos   Shawty Mane

Discography

Albums & EPs

My World (EP, 2009)

My World 2.0 (2010)

Under the Mistletoe (2011)

Believe (Forthcoming)

Singles

2009:   'One Time'

'One Less Lonely Girl'

2010:   'Baby' (feat. Ludacris, No. 1)

'Eenie Meenie' (feat. Sean Kingston)

'Never Let You Go'

'Somebody to Love'

'U Smile'

'Pray'

2011:   'Never Say Never'

'Mistletoe'

Awards
(including):

American Music Awards

2010:   Artist of the Year

Favorite Pop/Rock Male Artist

Favorite Pop/Rock Album (*My World 2.0*)

Billboard Music Awards

2011: Top New Artist

Top Social Artist

Top Streaming Artist

Top Digital Media Artist

Top Pop Album (*My World 2.0*)

Top Streaming Song (Video) ('Baby')

Brit Awards

2011: International Breakthrough Act

MTV Awards

2010: International Artist (MTV Video Music Brazil)

Best Push Act (MTV Europe)

Best New Artist (MTV Video Music Awards, 'Baby')

2011: Best Male (MTV Europe)

Best Pop (MTV Europe)

Best Male (MTV Video Music Awards, 'U Smile')

Best New Act (MTV Video Music Awards Japan)

Nickelodeon Kids' Choice Awards

2010: Hottest Hottie (Australian Kids' Choice)

2011: Favorite Male Singer (American Kids' Choice)

Favorite Song (American Kids' Choice, 'Baby')

Hottest Hottie (Australian Kids' Choice)

Teen Choice Awards

2010: Choice Music: Male Artist

Choice Music: Breakout Artist Male

Choice Summer Music Star: Male

Choice Music: Pop Album (*My World 2.0*)

2011: Choice Male Hottie

Choice Music: Male Artist

Online

justinbiebermusic.com:

Official site with merchandise, fanclubs, and the latest news

twitter.com/justinbieber:

Join the 15 million other followers at @justinbieber

facebook.com/JustinBieber:

Check out the Biebs' latest writing on the wall

myspace.com/justinbieber:

Look here for the lastest tracks

youtube.com/user/kidrauhl:

Where it all began: check out videos from 2007 to today

Biographies

Nadia Cohen (Author)

Nadia Cohen is an entertainment journalist who has worked at a number of national newspapers and magazines including *Grazia* and *The Daily Mail*. As a showbusiness correspondent she covered film festivals, premieres and award ceremonies around the world. Nadia was headhunted for the launch of a new American magazine, *In Touch Weekly*, and spent several years living and working in New York. *In Touch* now has a readership of over a million, while Nadia lives in London and juggles family life with showbiz news and gossip.

Mango Saul (Foreword)

Mango Saul has been a music, lifestyle and entertainment journalist for ten years. Some of his highlights include having breakfast at Waffle House with rapper Ludacris in Atlanta, sharing a bed with Destiny's Child for a *Smash Hits* cover interview and being sent an ice-cream costume for no reason. As Editor of Sugarscape.com, Mango has seen the site grow to over 4 million page views per month and was shortlisted for Digital Editorial Individual 2011 at the AOP Awards.

Picture Credits